UNITED STATES OF TRUE CRIME

The Most Chilling Cases In All 50 States

Arizona

Ashley Hudson

True Crime Publishing
Company LLC

ALSO BY ASHLEY HUDSON

Check out the entire *United States of True Crime* Series on Amazon. A new volume will be released every other month until all 50 states are complete:

https://www.amazon.com/dp/B09M3ZXV1Y?
binding=kindle_edition&ref=dbs_dp_rwt_sb_pc_tukn

Want to read or listen to the next book in the series for FREE?

We are constantly looking for readers to honestly review advance copies of our latest ebooks and audiobooks. If you'd like a free copy of the latest book in the *United States of True Crime* series, please send an email to freebooks@truecrimepublishingcompany.com or visit www.truecrimepublishingcompany.com and fill out the form to become part of our launch team and receive future books for free.

If you enjoy this book, I humbly ask that you take 30 seconds of your time to leave a review on Amazon at the below link I would greatly appreciate it:

https://www.amazon.com/gp/product/B09M1XMBP7?
ref_=dbs_m_mng_rwt_calw_tkin_0&storeType=ebooks

CONTENTS

NOTES FROM THE AUTHOR

As the title of this book implies, the following ten chapters depict true crimes—and it's not for everyone. These true stories include accounts of hate crimes and racial injustice, alcoholism, poisoning, sex work, mental illness, child abuse, animal abuse, bombs, shooting sprees, abduction, sexual assault and abuse, suicide, feticide, murders of children and adults, mutilation, and necrophilia. I've tried to cover these cases in a way that dignifies the victims and their families, but the reality of these crimes includes topics that may not be appropriate for everyone.

Great care has gone into researching various sources for each of these cases. When sources conflict, I've done my best to analyze all available information and present a narrative that represents the truth as supported by reputable media coverage. I hope you enjoy reading these true stories and maybe even recognize behaviors that could save you or your loved ones from being a victim in the future.

INTRODUCTION

The Grand Canyon State is known for its natural beauty. A place visitors come to bask in the sun while soaking in the scenery of saguaros, colorful petrified wood, and, of course, the awe-inspiring vastness of the Grand Canyon.

Despite the beautiful sunny climate, some chilling crimes have happened throughout the state's history. This book will serve as a guide to some of the most notorious crimes in Arizona history.

In 2020, USA Today ranked Arizona the nation's tenth-worst state for violent crime, at a rate of 474.9 out of 100,000. Depressed areas nationwide typically see higher crime rates, and Arizona's poverty rate hovers around 14-percent—that's the nation's 14th highest.

In a report by the Arizona Department of Public safety, Arizona saw 28,777 violent crimes in 2020, including 423 murders, 19,751 assaults, and 2,838 instances of reported rape. A violent crime was reported every 18 minutes and 16 seconds. Another surprising statistic is that almost 57% percent of the murders were committed using a handgun.

But enough numbers. The victims have names and stories, and so do the perpetrators. In these pages, you'll meet some of the most depraved criminals as we attempt to understand what may have driven several of Arizona's most chilling crimes.

In reviewing the cases for this book, a troubling pattern of domestic violence surfaced. While some cases were perpetrated by the terrifying stranger lurking in the shadows, four of these cases involved the murder of a family member or roommate. Although it is not always common, in these cases, the warning signs were there; red flags of abuse were obvious to the extended family and friends of the victims prior to the crimes. I can only hope that sharing these stories will encourage those who need help to escape abusive situations to seek it, and maybe we can prevent future tragedies. Resources such as the National Domestic Violence Hotline are available at a federal level. State-specific resources like the Domestic Violence Services page on the Arizona Department of Economic Security's website provide resources in county-specific formats for anyone seeking help.

This tour will introduce you to multiple serial killers terrorizing the greater Phoenix area simultaneously, a scorned lover who snapped, a pedophile who preyed upon multiple young girls, a family annihilator, plus more ruthless killers. And you'll meet their victims, too.

You will notice that not all of the cases included in this book are the most violent in state history. While serial murderers are included, I've also included some cases that are unsettling because of the gnawing sense of injustice they leave.

Subsequent chapters will reveal some of Arizona's most heartless criminals and the victim and their families whose lives will be forever changed. As always, we hope to honor and remember all of the victims. Without the clues they revealed to investigators, often after death, the monsters who preyed on them would likely have continued to walk among us. While the cases could not have been solved without the careful attention of law enforcement, it's truly the victims who are the heroes in the true stories you'll now read.

WINNIE RUTH JUDD

The case of the famous "Trunk Murders" and the convicted murderess Winnie Ruth Judd is such an outlandish tale that it's been the subject of multiple best-selling books, podcasts, and movies. Almost a century after the murders, the public is still fascinated.

October 19, 1931, at the Los Angeles train station, a baggage handler, H.C. Mapes, noticed a foul odor and some fluids leaking from the various containers. He located the owner, 25-year-old Winnie Ruth Judd, known to friends as Ruth, and requested that she open the case; Judd excused herself to go and retrieve the key. Mapes, meanwhile, did not open the trunks because deer meat was frequently smuggled by rail from place to place in those days, so he waited for his supervisor Arthur V. Anderson to actually make the gruesome discovery.

In an unexpected twist, the scent emanating from the trunks was that of decomposition, though not of an animal. Upon opening the luggage, officials discovered the remains of two young women. One, hacked to pieces that were distributed within large steamer trunks, a (smaller) valise, and even a hatbox; the second corpse stuffed, intact, into a large trunk.

Officials inspecting the blood-stained trunks

Authorities soon discovered that Judd, who had traveled from Phoenix with the two bodies, had left the station with her brother Burton McKinnell, then slipped away somewhere in downtown L.A.

While searching for Judd, an investigation into her life revealed a steamy love triangle, very taboo for the time. Despite being married, the young woman was in a relationship with a local businessman, Jack Halloran. It appeared that Judd's former roommates Hedvig "Sammy" Samuelson, and Agnes Anne LeRoi, were also romantically involved with Halloran. Law enforcement were able to positively identify the bodies as Samuelson and LeRoi.

Hedving "Sammy" Samuelson   Agnes Anne LeRoi

The 1931 media went wild. Judd's face was splashed across newspapers nationwide, leading her to turn herself into Los Angeles police one week after the bodies were discovered. The public couldn't get enough of the salacious story.

Jack Halloran, 44, had been engaged in an extramarital affair with Judd, who was twenty years younger than him, and was well known as a leading playboy and philanderer in the city. He was involved with city politics and Phoenix's up-and-coming social scene. Despite his denial of any involvement in the murders, he could not deny that his gray Packard was seen at the scene of the crime – the bungalow that Samuelson and LeRoi shared as housemates and where Judd had also lived, although she had moved out due to discord among the three women.

Judd had said that she often felt like a third wheel between the women, implying their relationship was more than a friendship. Regardless, in an arrangement unthinkable to most at the time, all three women were also openly dating Halloran. He showered them with gifts and seduced them with his playboy lifestyle. All the women were presumably content until Judd introduced Jack to a fourth woman.

Jack Halloran

The story, according to Judd, is that she went over to her friends' bungalow and tempers flared. She alleges that the two women teamed up against her, and that Samuelson attacked her, wielding a .25 caliber pistol while LeRoi hit her over the head with an ironing board. In the scuffle, Judd received a gunshot wound to her hand before gaining control of the weapon and shooting the two women. Until her death, Judd maintained that her actions were in self-defense and that she did not mutilate the bodies.

Despite her version of events, there are still numerous unanswered questions surrounding the case, such as who dismembered the bodies and who had the idea that Judd should travel with the bodies by train to Los Angeles? Did Judd and Halloran act together, or did Halloran help Judd escape after discovering she had shot her two friends?

Investigators were never satisfied that such a slight woman was capable of hauling the dead weight of two of her friends and cutting clean through the spine of one of them, all on her own. Severing the spine of an adult human is a difficult task that many thought could only be performed by a doctor, leading to an even more interesting theory number three. Did Halloran commit the murders, then call on a friend named Dr. Brown, to help dismember Samuelson's body? In a letter to the LA Times years later, it was revealed that an associate of Halloran's, Dr. Brown, had made an appointment with a judge to discuss the case before committing suicide just one day before the meeting. It is possible that Dr. Brown might have been the one to butcher one of the bodies after being blackmailed by a prominent man like Halloran. Did "Happy Jack" then call his 25-year-old ingenue and ask her to transport the trunks?

Halloran was, indeed, indicted in December 1932, just as Judd's trial was nearing completion. She was tried for the murder of Agnes Anne LeRoi, the woman whose body was still intact, so the subject of dismembering a body was not discussed during the trial. No one was ever brought to trial for the murder of Hedvig Samuelson.

Judd was found guilty of LeRoi's murder on February 8, 1933, and sentenced to be hanged nine days later on February 17. Jack was indicted on December 30, and the chief witness at the hearing was Winnie Ruth Judd, who had just attempted to avoid prison by claiming she was insane. Judd testified for three days, but Halloran's attorney dismissed the context of her testimony, claiming an insane woman could not be trusted to tell the truth. The judge called the evidence against him inconsistent, and Halloran was released.

Halloran's shadow falls on the case in a second manner that demonstrates the influence a wealthy businessman could wield during the Great Depression. It came to light soon after Judd was sentenced to be hanged that four jurors in sworn affidavits said that the mayor of Mesa, a man named Dave Kleinman, had convinced the jurors to vote for the death penalty. Kleinman argued that the threat of capital punishment would pressure Judd into confessing.

Winnie "Ruth" Judd in jail

Despite the affidavits that Kleinman had manipulated the jury in a sentencing hearing, the court ruled the hanging sentence was valid. However, soon after this, Judd was deemed in hindsight, incompetent to stand trial, so her sentence was commuted to life spent at Arizona's only state mental hospital.

Judd escaped from the Arizona State Asylum of the Insane six times during her sentence. In her final escape, in 1963, she made it to San Francisco, where she changed her name to Marian Kane and worked as a domestic servant for a wealthy family. She was caught six years later and returned to the hospital.

Upon her reincarceration, Judd retained lawyers Larry Debus and Melvin Belli to petition for her freedom. After two years, the attorneys secured a pardon from Governor Jack Williams. When Judd was released in December 1971, she went back to California to work for the same family.

After Judd's arrest hit the newspapers, the landlord of the bungalow where the women were slain, placed an ad in two newspapers – The Arizona Republic and The Phoenix Evening Gazette – offering tours of the home for 10 cents per person. Hundreds of people showed up to gawk at the crime scene, which created one of the more polluted crime scenes in the annals of due process. "By the advertisements in the newspapers, the entire population of Maricopa County visited that place," Judd's attorney complained during the trial.

Even today, questions need to be asked. Was Judd a star-crossed young lover who did Happy Jack Halloran a solid and took the fall for the Trunk Murders? Investigative journalist Jana Bommersbach in her 1992 book "The Trunk Murderess Winnie Ruth Judd" concluded that Judd did not have the skills or strength to lift the bodies of the victims or to surgically carve up Hedvig Samuelson, which required a practiced hand to do as neatly as investigators had discovered. Judd also said that a Dr. Brown had visited her in the Arizona State Prison and confessed that he had taken part in the crime and would soon divulge the truth. A nurse named Ann Miller corroborated this story.

In a letter obtained by Phoenix's CBS 5, Ruth Judd kept the mystery of her case alive, denying any involvement after she shot the women. The letter reads:

"I was not present when dismemberment, and the bodies placed in the trunks, took place. I had always lived a Christian life, and I am still a Christian. I have always contended my innocence of murder.

There have been many statements I supposedly made such as I shot myself trying to commit suicide, and that I made a confession to murder. If I did make such statements, I have no knowledge of them. I am confessing to shooting Sammy and Anne, but never will I confess to murder — only self-defense."

The murders would have occurred on an ironically pleasant

evening after an ironically pleasant day in Phoenix in 1931, which then had a population of 48,000 residents. It would be the same weather that would have greeted Judd when she returned to Phoenix to finish out her life. After her work with the wealthy family ended, Judd lived in Stockton, California. She had been released from the asylum in December 1971, and granted "absolute discharge" in 1983, giving her freedom to live where she pleased. After Stockton, she moved back to Phoenix, where she died exactly 67 years to the day she turned herself in to the Los Angeles Police Department. On October 23, 1998, she died at age 93, taking any clues regarding how the bodies ended up in the trunks with her.

MARK GOUDEAU

Phoenix, Arizona, is a thriving, modern desert community of 1.6 million residents all of them living in what is ranked as the sunniest major city on the planet. That includes those blue-sky meccas in Egypt, Namibia, the Middle East – anywhere at all.

But in a 13-month reign of terror, Phoenix became one of the world's most frightening places on Earth, as it became the home of not one, but two vicious serial killing episodes that, in the end, were found to be the work of three men.

The nightmare started in mid-2005 when police began receiving reports of multiple fatalities in drive-by-style shootings, mostly at night. People, and even animals, were the targets of the seemingly random violence. The media dubbed this killer the "Serial Shooter," and this shooter terrorized the area throughout the following year.

In August of 2005, the violence in Phoenix escalated with the beginning of another series of attacks in which an assailant began preying upon women and young girls in brutal sexual assaults. This predator was dubbed the "Baseline Rapist."

On September 9, the body of 19-year-old Georgia Thompson was found outside her Tempe apartment. Although her pants were unzipped, it was determined that she was not sexually assaulted. She likely resisted her attacker and paid the price with her life. She was executed via a gunshot to her head. There is a sad irony to Georgia's death because she had recently moved to Arizona from Idaho, seeking a brighter future. At this point, the Baseline Rapist became the Baseline Killer.

Georgia Thompson

Authorities were alerted to the point that the Baseline Rapist was quickly becoming unhinged. Crime sprees often escalate in nature, and already, the Baseline Rapist had added armed robbery and homicide to his repertoire. Just seven days later, on September 15, at 9:40 a.m., another sexual assault occurred. This time the attack was in a residential section of the city, indicating that the Baseline Rapist was finding his urge to rape and kill impossible to control, as he was willing to trade in the cover of night for a crime occurring in broad daylight.

The predator continued his vicious assaults, brutally murdering anyone who dared to resist him. In the following months, it seemed that no one was safe. While the Serial Shooter continued his murder spree, the frequency of the sexual assaults increased. Police surmised that these two killers were engaged in a sort of depraved competition, fueling each to commit more violent acts.

As the brutality intensified, even women who stayed in pairs were vulnerable to this attacker. On September 20, two sisters, one of whom was visibly pregnant, were sexually assaulted. The next week, on September 28, a mother and daughter were abducted and both were sexually assaulted. The offender was growing increasingly bold after each successful attack. The rashness of his behavior was also evident in his indifference to targeting women even when a male accompanied them. Two murders occurred on the night of March 15, 2006; the incident began when 20-year-old Liliana Sanchez-Cabrera ended her first day at her first job at a fast-food restaurant (Yoshi's) on 24th Street and Indian School Road. Before she got very far, she was offered a ride home from a co-worker named Chao "George" Chou.

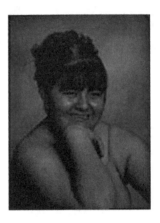

Liliana Sanchez-Cabrera

However, the bodies of both were later found, each killed by gunshots to the head, their bodies found a mile apart. According to the article "Summer of Fear: A Timeline of Events" in The Republic, it was at this point that law enforcement realized the violence plaguing the city was the work of two separate offenders.

Fear permeated all of Phoenix after the murder of Carmen Miranda on June 29, 2006, was caught on camera. At 9:30 p.m., Carmen chatted with her boyfriend while she vacuumed her car at a well-lit, seemingly safe, car wash. She mentioned that a panhandler was approaching her, abruptly crying out before the line went dead. Her boyfriend sprang into action, calling police and immediately mobilizing a search party of family members. Unfortunately, regardless of the swift response, Carmen's body was found just hours later, less than a mile from where she was abducted. In a break for police, they were able to obtain surveillance footage of the attack. The grainy footage depicted a light-skinned Black man in a cartoonish disguise, dreadlocks, and a "Gilligan-style" hat, efficiently approaching Miranda and forcing her into the back of her car before driving off. The whole encounter lasted only a few seconds. When the media broadcast the footage, the brutality instilled public panic.

Carmen Miranda

Needless to say, the city of Phoenix at this point was horrified, and each week seemed to reveal more of this continuous rampage. More than this, it was learned by ABC-15 News that the police still had ten persons of interest on their suspect list.

The police, however, were banking on the public's help in solving the Baseline Killer's assault on the city. They attended or held numerous community meetings to distribute police sketches of the assailant rendered from survivor's account and posted a $100,000 reward for leads that resulted in the arrest and conviction of the Baseline Killer. Even then, it took another year after these outreach efforts began for a suspect to be arrested in the case. That's a long time for a community to be aware a serial killer is out there, especially one who it seems is targeting all types of people, at all times of day, seemingly at random.

Police sketch of the Baseline Killer

Arizonians were finally able to breathe a sigh of relief when the long-awaited arrest occurred on September 6, 2006, with the original charges related to the sexual assault of two sisters who survived their attack – the assault that included one victim who was visibly pregnant when the attack occurred. According to court testimony later given regarding the attack, the attacker used a condom but was physically unable to complete the sex act. At the time of the attack, police were not hopeful that they would be able to retrieve DNA evidence as there was no semen present. Nevertheless, after a full year of testing, analysts were eventually able to extract DNA from the offender's saliva left on the breast of the victim who was not pregnant. The testing had been severely delayed after the rapist ordered both women to spit into his hand; he rubbed their saliva and a bit of dirt on top of his saliva in a feeble attempt to destroy evidence.

On the evening of his 42nd birthday, Mark Goudeau was arrested at his Phoenix home. Initially, Godeau was only charged in connection with the September 2005 sexual assaults, but police were diligently gathering forensic evidence to connect him to all of the Baseline Rapist attacks.

After the Goudeau arrest, there was significant blowback, including from his wife, friends, and co-workers who denied that Goudeau could ever be a serial killer. His wife, Wendy Carr, told reporters, "My husband is innocent," calling the arrest "a huge miscarriage of justice."

"He shouldn't be in jail for something he didn't do," she told the Associated Press.

Mark Goudeau

Goudeau, it turns out, was a docile man at home known for taking great care maintaining his property, especially his front lawn. His wife described him as a loving man.

Police countered that picture, noting that Goudeau was an ex-convict whose previous arrests were for rape and kidnapping. However, he negotiated a plea deal which resulted in a conviction for aggravated assault. He was convicted to 21 years in prison but was released after only serving 13 years. During the Baseline Killer's reign of terror, Goudeau was on parole.

Ultimately Mark Goudeau was charged with 74 crimes, including nine counts of first-degree murder, ten counts of kidnapping, twelve counts of armed robbery, and four counts of attempted armed robbery. Among the charges that were sexual in nature were five counts of sexual assault, three counts of attempted sexual assault, three counts of sexual abuse, nine counts of sexual conduct with a minor, and three counts of indecent exposure.

After a highly publicized trial, the jury delivered 67 guilty verdicts, including all of the murders police attributed to the Baseline Killer. This resulted in a sentencing of 438 years in prison, which would be somewhat moot, given he was also sentenced to death nine times.

If that wasn't enough, in a second trial stemming from the incident where Goudeau sexually assaulted the two sisters at gunpoint, he was convicted of 19 additional crimes. This put the total of years in prison he was sentenced to serve at 1,634.

Even after it was determined that Mark Goudeau would never again be free to terrorize the public, some extremely troubling details of the Baseline Killer case, will haunt psychologists, police, and the public for the rest of time. Just for starters, the Baseline Killer's documented crime spree began with two sexual assaults in an incident in which he forced three teenagers at gunpoint on August 5, 2005, at 9:46 in the evening behind a church, where he sexually assaulted two of the girls. Eight days later, on August 14, documents show Goudeau perpetrated a combined armed robbery, sexual assault at 4:10 a.m. and on September 8, the first documented homicide occurred.

How did a rapist/murderer justify or rationalize his move to daytime crimes? In another haunting dimension to this case, the Baseline Rapist/Killer had decided to start wearing disguises. In an incident occurring November 5, the Baseline Rapist/Killer appeared wearing dreadlocks and a fisherman's hat when he robbed a store at gunpoint, taking $720 from the cash register. Less than 10 minutes after this, the same man sexually assaulted a woman in her car, his face hiding behind a Halloween mask and plastic glasses. After assaulting this woman, he demanded she drive him down the street, so he could escape, saying he had just committed a robbery.

Victims and witnesses after this reported suspects in Baseline Killer incidents in a variety of disguises. In some incidents, the Baseline Killer, was reported to have long black hair, while in other incidents he was reported to be bald. In the August 14 combined sexual assault and robbery, a man pushing a shopping cart, who appeared to be homeless, used the cart to entrap a woman and force her into her car, where he demanded oral sex and threatened to kill her. By this point, Mark Goudeau was using gloves and wearing a long-sleeved shirt to conceal his identity but also to ensure few samples of dander or scrapped off skin cells would provide forensic investigators with organic evidence containing DNA. Was he aware of incriminating DNA evidence? Certainly, he was. During his sexual assaults, the Baseline Rapist always used condoms.

Shortly after Goudeau's arrest, the waters were muddied slightly when Kentucky police reported that suspect James Dewayne Mullins, arrested for robbery, confessed to the September 8, 2005 murder of a woman named Georgia Thompson, who was thought to be the third Baseline Killer victim. Over time, however, the Mullins confession appeared more and more disjointed, and some of the evidence he revealed did not match up. Interest in his confession quickly faded away.

While it seems understandable that wrongful convictions, even in murder cases, do occur, the idea that a man could be wrongfully convicted of 67 felonies, including nine murders, requires a leap of distrust that is hard to fathom. Police say ballistic evidence, forensic evidence, DNA evidence, and circumstantial evidence all point to the arrest and conviction of the right man. Yet, DNA evidence presented at the trial, described as being accurate by a factor of 360 trillion, was later described as containing only 3 of 13 possible genetic markers for a fully qualified match.

In a further frustrating twist, several years later, in April 2009, a regional publication from Phoenix, Time Publication, released a story that said DNA evidence had been in police possession nine months before Goudeau's arrest, but they had not had the evidence analyzed until it was too late to stop the murder spree. Many wondered how many lives could have been spared if the analysis had been done sooner.

Nonetheless, while Mark Goudeau waits on death row, a second suspect in the Baseline Rapist/Killler case emerged in June 2009, when a police report revealed a man fitting the description of the Baseline Killer, who lived in the vicinity of the crimes and had a long, violent track record in California and Arizona. Some wondered if this man could have been an accomplice. CBS 5 and reporter Tammy Leitner investigated the possible connection and reported that the other suspect's DNA was tested, and it could not be positively linked to any of the Baseline attacks.

Despite DNA linking Godeau to the crimes, he still maintains his innocence. In Leitner's article, when asked about the possible accomplice, Goudeau said, "I don't know if he's the right guy, but I know I'm not the right guy."

SAMUEL DIETEMAN
& DALE HAUSNER

There is no question that the crime spree of Samuel Dieteman and Dale Hausner from the summer of 2005 through the summer of 2006 in the Mesa/Phoenix area had appallingly depraved dimensions. This pair of methamphetamine users gleefully murdered at least eight persons in what one of the assailants, Dieteman defined as "random recreational violence." By the time they were through, Hausner, considered the "mastermind" of the destruction, was convicted of 80 out of 87 felony charges he faced, including five murders. He was sentence to six death penalties, while his partner in crime, Samuel Dieteman was convicted of two murders and, because he rolled over on Dale Hausner and his brother, Jeff, he was allowed to live, but given two life sentences.

Dale's brother Jeff was convicted of attempted murder and aggravated assault and given sentences of fourteen and nine years, respectively, for stabbing 36-year-old Timothy Davenport several times in the back. His brother Dale first distracted Davenport so Jeff Hausner could sneak up on him.

This all began in May 2005 when Dieteman and Dale Hausner, high on meth, went cruising in Dale Hausner's light blue Toyota Camry looking for a good time. What they considered fun was drive-by shootings. They began by taking shots at animals, including one horse and several dogs. Then, by June 29, they graduated to shooting people, killing 20-year-old David Estrada in a drive-by, the first of their murders that were proved in court.

David Estrada with his sister

A September 2, 2016 staff report from AZ Central commented on the evolving violence, "Then there were immigrants on bicycles, transients sleeping on benches in west Phoenix or panhandling under an overpass in Tolleson, all of them shot dead with .22-caliber slugs."

Their victims also included Nathaniel Shoffner, 44, murdered while bravely trying to protect a dog from being killed.

Moreover, as discussed in the Mark Goudeau chapter, the months from May 2005 to June 2006 included not one but two serial killing sprees in the city of Phoenix, each with very different M-Os, but each of them overlapping month by month, starting and ending in close proximity.

Aside from the callous attitudes of the two Serial Killers, Hausner and Dieteman, is the unfathomable point that on two occasions, June 29 to November 11, 2005 and December 19, 2005 to May 2, 2006, the pair stopped their murderous rampage for five months, then started up again. This might make sense from a psychological point of view if a single shooter was involved, but two murderers both agreeing it was time to get back to murdering after a five-month hiatus is beyond understanding.

Paul Patrick

In addition, there was the night of December 29, moving into the morning of December 30, 2005. In the course of five and a half hours, in an extraordinary rampage, Hausner and Dieteman began with a drive-by shooting near a bartending school. The pair then took a tour of central Phoenix, murdering a dog that was being walked by its owner, then killing two men, Jose Ortis and Marco Carillo. Just a few moments after this, Timmy Tordai was shot and paralyzed for life with the bullet entering just under his collarbone.

Three more dogs were shot and killed that night, and then, shortly after midnight, the pair shot another woman who miraculously survived.

Another of Hausner and Dieteman's victims, near the end of their crime career, Paul Patrick, was also gravely wounded, shot while he was headed to a mini-mall to buy a pack of cigarettes. Called out of his nearby house by his mother, Army National Guard corpsman Saul Geuerroro, an Iraq war veteran, grabbed a gun and a first aid kit and ran to his assistance, barefoot and without a shirt, then helped Patrick hold his intestines in place, until the ambulance arrived. Patrick lived, but lost the ability to walk and suffered horrendous medical complications for the rest of his life.

By then, Hausner and Dieteman had taken another step to prove the unparalleled level of depravity that governed their lives. They had switched to using a shotgun, after learning that there is no way to do a forensic analysis of a shotgun pellet that can match the ammunition to the gun, unlike the previously used .22-caliber slugs.

In addition, on June 8, the pair added arson to their list of "recreational violence," setting fires in two different Wal-Marts about 45 minutes apart. The first fire resulted in $7 million in damage, while the second caused $10 million worth of destruction.

Perhaps the most regrettable aspect of this violent spree was that before their methamphetamine addictions, Hausner and Dieteman had only committed petty crimes, nothing to indicate they were capable of the level of the atrocity of the serial shooting rampage.

Before the "summer of violence", Dale Shawn Hausner, 33, worked as a custodian at the Phoenix Sky Harbor International Airport. He was also a photojournalist who specialized in boxing events, working for RingSports and Fightnews.com. On the side, during his day job, he ran a shoplift-to-order business, stealing items like alcohol and cigarettes, then selling them to co-workers for a discounted price.

Samuel John Dieteman, 31, was a trained electrician, who could not hold a job due to his drug and alcohol addictions. His vainglorious rap sheet prior to helping his buddy murder at least eight people and wound 29, involved that grab-bag of mischief called "petty crime."

Dale Hausner   Samuel Dieteman

Depravity is also measured by the level of care a criminal takes in not getting caught. Every step taken to cover up a crime, erase clues, and throw authorities off the trail is another realization that the criminals know what they are doing wrong. At one point during the investigation, 375 Phoenix police officers were assigned to the case, with another 100 officers working the Baseline Killer case. While police worked overtime week after week, they held community meetings to warn residents, seek information, and assure the public they were focusing all of their efforts on stopping the killers. A $100,000 reward was posted for each of the serial killers – as the Serial Shooter was long thought to be the work of one perpetrator.

Still, no description of the Serial Shooter was forthcoming. Police knew only that the shooter drove a light-colored four-door sedan. They had yet to identify the car as a light-blue Toyota Camry until after the tip came in that led to the arrest of the two Hausners and Samuel Dieteman.

That tip came on July 31, 2006 after Dieteman confessed his involvement in the crimes to a friend while the two were drinking in a Mesa bar called the Star Dust Inn. Motivated by the $100,000 reward, that friend quickly betrayed Dieteman.

The last killing by the Serial Shooter occurred on July 30, when a young woman was walking through her neighborhood in Mesa, feeling so safe, one report said, that Robin Blasnek was wearing pajamas at the time she was killed.

But from the time Dieteman's friend Ron Horton called the police to the time of the arrests on August 2 is one of those intense episodes in law enforcement that some participants say they will never forget.

It began with Horton calling the police, at which point he gave them Dieteman's name and telephone number, plus the name of Horton's former roommate Jeff Hausner, Dale's younger brother.

The police quickly traced Dieteman's phone. Then they asked Horton to invite Dieteman to join him for drinks the next day.

Jeff Hausner

The next day, like a scene from a movie, police had the Star Dust Inn fully staked out with undercover officers inside the bar and outside, some in unmarked cars. That's when Jeff Hausner showed up with Sam Dieteman in the vehicle they had been seeking for almost a year. Running the car's license plates, they found it was owned by Dale Hausner, a name that until that point was unconnected to the case.

Hausner, meanwhile, drove to the Metrocenter Mall, where police attached a GPS device to his car. Simultaneously Horton, the informant, drove Dieteman to another bar, the Wild Horse Pass Hotel and Casino. Horton headed home, leaving Dieteman there to wait for his buddy, Dale Hausner.

After Hausner showed up, the two had drinks, then headed out to Hausner's car. When they got there, they opened the trunk and pulled out a long package that was the size and length of a shotgun. Then they drove away.

No less than eleven vehicles trailed the pair, including air support, but no arrests were made. Instead, the police tailed the two Serial Shooters while they drove in a random pattern through Phoenix neighborhoods, making unexpected turns and U-turns. It was evident to every officer who followed that the duo was on the hunt, cruising around to find their next victim. Without sufficient evidence for an arrest, officers helplessly tailed the car.

Detective Clark Schwartzkopf later described that night as "the worst night of my law-enforcement career." Throughout the pursuit, police rolled down their windows and yelled to pedestrians to get off the street and take cover. While gathering evidence to make their arrests, officers had to follow along, suspecting that at any minute the shotgun would appear in a car window, and someone would be dead.

Out of sheer luck, perhaps, the Serial Shooters did not brandish their shotgun that night, although for an hour and a half, a lot of Phoenix and Mesa law enforcement officers aged noticeably.

Finally, at 11:00 p.m. that night, officers had enough information to press criminal judge James Keppel to issue a warrant for an emergency wiretap. At this point, police used a listening device set up from the neighbor's apartment. The results were chilling.

They heard Dieteman repeating something about the Serial Shooter noting the latest murder of a young woman had been identified as a serial killer shooting. The men were listening to a news report that put the death toll at six, and Hausner corrected that. He said they got it wrong. The number was eight.

When the report said that other states were looking at similar crime sprees, Hausner chillingly remarked "We're leading the way for a better life for everybody, Sam."

The two also talked about how much pleasure they got shooting people in the back. "That's so much fun," Hausner said. Meanwhile, as this conversation continued, police could also hear the television in the background. It was Hausner's young daughter, a toddler, watching "Jungle Book" on television.

Late that night, the arrests were made. When Samuel Dieteman took a bag of trash to the dumpster, police grabbed him. He then gave officers the keys to the apartment. They snuck up on Hausner and arrested him, too.

With so much rampant destruction, mayhem, and ugly violence, it took until March 2009 for Hausner to be convicted. He received six death penalty sentences. By then, Hausner's remorse had caught up with him. After the mandatory appeal, he instructed his attorneys to waive his rights for any more appeals. Guards found him unconscious in his cell on September 2, 2016, from an overdose of antidepressants. He died that night, never regaining consciousness.

In a "too little, too late" apology, Dale Hausner had asked for his execution to take place "as soon as possible," saying only his death would give the grieving families some closure.

Samuel Dieteman is currently serving two life sentences without the possibility of parole.

CORY DEONN MORRIS

On the surface, the case of Cory Deonn Morris, born in Oklahoma City in May 1978, resembles the plot of a made-for-TV movie with a kind yet troubled murderer living in plain sight, working at a neighborhood bar, and camped out in a trailer in his aunt and uncle's backyard in Phoenix, Arizona.

Morris, known as the Crackhead Killer, was described by his boss at the Fat Cat Lounge as a considerate man who came to work early, was always the last to leave, and took out the garbage so his female co-workers wouldn't have to venture outside the bar at night. According to an article in the Oklahoman, co-workers even affectionately referred to Morris as "Huggy Bear" because "he was so nice."

Cory Deonn Morris

In his youth, he was described as a sweet kid who got good grades and joined the Reserved Officers Training Corp while still in high school. He was the oldest of three children, raised by a single mother but very little else is known of his childhood, except that the only trouble in his early years involved a BB gun and a streetlight. This hardly constitutes a troubled youth. Morris was even noted for helping distribute food and taking part in other volunteer work after the famous April 19, 1995 bombing of the Alfred P. Murrah Federal Building in his hometown.

But the Cory Morris case is also the story of a serial killer who sunk to the depths of depravity by luring sex workers to the recreational trailer where he lived in his uncle's backyard in the Garfield District of Phoenix. He paid them for sex, then strangled them while they were having intercourse. Later, with all but one of his victims – there are thought to be six, although he was only convicted for five – Morris continued to have intercourse with the corpses, at one point leaving the corpse in his bed for three days after the woman's death.

When he was asked if he committed acts of necrophilia, Morris said he masturbated beside the corpse, but that his back was facing the corpse. He also said he used a condom during sexual contact while the women were alive yet, there is forensic evidence refuting Morris' claims after semen matching his DNA was collected from several of his victims' bodies.

Morris likely got away with his crimes for so long because all of his victims had a history of serious drug abuse, and one had the intellectual capacity of a nine-to-eleven-year-old. Initially, when his first victims were discovered, toxicology reports confirmed the presence of cocaine. Law enforcement was slow to determine that the women were murdered, initially suspecting a bad batch of drugs.

After his arrest, Morris gave two versions concerning the death of each of the victims, one that involved drug overdoses and a second version in which each of them asked him to choke her during intercourse.

Morris declined the courts request that he undergo both IQ and psychiatric evaluations prior to trial, which accounts for the lack of details about his childhood and the limited insights about how that affected his life. The murders all occurred in 2002-2003 when Morris was 24-years old.

His life was certainly marginalized at this time. His job: He worked three nights a week running the karaoke machine at a bar, which was a popular hangout for sex workers and pimps. But Morris' acts would not seem to be his response to depression or despair.

All five bodies were found within two blocks of his camper and his final victim, Julie Castillo was found under a blanket in the camper after his uncle noticed a rotting smell and saw a window of the camper covered in flies. When he looked inside, he found the floor of the camper "boiling" with flies and maggots and the dead body under a blanket.

Janice Alvern was the first victim found and the storyline reveals a murderer who made only the most cursory efforts to cover his tracks. Morris kept a few souvenirs, including her underwear and some other clothes, then took her nude body and put it in a shopping cart. He dumped the body in a nearby alley and repeated this pattern four more times.

One striking difference in the cases involved Jade Velazquez, who Morris considered a friend. Before dumping her body, he put her clothing back on, thinking it inconsiderate to leave her in an alley completely nude.

The other victims were Barbara Codman in September 2002, Shanteria Davis in October 2002, and Sherry Noah in March 2003. The body of Janice Alvern was similarly found in April 2002, but that case was not included in Morris' trial.

Even the stories Morris told followed a distinct pattern. In each case, he claimed the victims agreed to go to his camper and have sex with him, often for very small fees - $5 in one of the cases. He then claimed he would leave the women alone because they wanted to do drugs, after which he would find them unconscious or in an early stage of an overdose. Then he would leave – either to go to work or to a friend's – and return the next day or some hours later to find they had not regained consciousness.

All the police had to do to get Morris to change his story was tell them they didn't believe him. The second versions of the stories, however, were offered with paint-by-numbers consistency. In each of the cases, Morris then said, the women asked him to choke her during sex and in all of the cases he did not realize they were unconscious until it was too late.

Obviously, the jury did not believe Morris was simply caught in a déjà vu of mishaps. He was sentenced to death five times and his appeals were denied.

Morris' appeals were based on the legal doctrine of corpus delicti, which governs the notion that one cannot assume a crime has been committed without proof. Morris claimed that strangulation could not be proved as the cause of death. Doctors could not find evidence of forceful strangulation because the bodies had decomposed too much for the trauma to be documented. Given the length of time Morris kept the bodies, it was assumed that he was deriving pleasure from the smell of the rotting bodies. The smell of decomposition was said to be so overpowering on Morris that even after he was away from his trailer for hours, co-workers and friends commented on his aroma. One can only imagine how much he must have interacted with the corpses to attain that level of filth.

Despite only ever being tried and convicted for the murders in Arizona, some wonder if this monster should be linked to other cases. In the previously mentioned article from the Oklahoman, journalists Ken Raymond and Greg Elwell introduce the idea that Corey Morris may be responsible for four other unsolved homicides. It is entirely possible that given Morris' ties to Oklahoma, his killings in Arizona may not have been his first. The article lists four cases of known sex workers with drug addictions, aligning perfectly with Morris' victimology, whose nude bodies were found. Two of the women in Oklahoma were confirmed to have high levels of cocaine in their system at the time of their deaths; the other two were too severely decomposed for analysis. All four women, Janice Marie Buono, Mandy Ann Raite, Cassandra Lee Ramsey, and Jane Marie Chafton are still listed on the Oklahoma State Bureau of Investigation's website as unsolved homicides.

As of this writing, all of Morris' appeals have failed. He is currently a kitchen worker at the Arizona Department of Corrections Florence Unit, waiting for his death sentences to be carried out.

ROBERT FISHER

A triple homicide from 2001 still haunts the state of Arizona and the Scottsdale neighborhood where it occurred. On the morning of April 10 at 8:42 a.m., police responded to an explosion at the home of the Fisher family. After extinguishing the blaze, the bodies of 38-year-old Mary Fisher, 10-year-old Bobby, and 12-year-old Brittney were identified. Law enforcement was unable to locate the father of the family, Robert.

Fisher home ablaze

Initially, it appeared that the family may have been the unlucky victims of a gas leak, but upon investigation, it quickly became apparent that something much more sinister had occurred. Investigators discovered that the fire was not the family's cause of death; rather, it was a forensic countermeasure to conceal the truth.

The coroner determined that the two children and Mary Fisher died between 9:30 and 10:10 p.m. on the night *before* the explosion. All their throats had been slashed, and Mary received a gunshot wound to the back of the head, after she was already dead.

Robert, Mary, Brittney, and Bobby Fisher

Police concluded that the explosion was a carefully orchestrated diversion that gave the perpetrator a ten-hour head start. After slaying the family, the killer poured an accelerant throughout the house, including dousing the three bodies together in bed in an upstairs bedroom. Then the perpetrator pulled a gas line off the furnace, allowing the home to slowly fill up with gas. Gas, of course, is lighter than air, so it floats to the ceiling. To delay the explosion, the perpetrator lit a candle and placed it on the floor, ensuring the gas wouldn't reach the flame until the rooms were nearly full of gas. According to neighbors, the blast shook homes a half-mile in all directions.

Days after the death of his family made headlines, Robert Fisher was still nowhere to be found. When police considered the deeply personal nature of the murders, combined with the fact that Robert was a former firefighter who would have known how to rig an explosion, he became their number one suspect.

In the hours after his family was murdered, the athletic-looking Robert Fisher appeared on an ATM surveillance camera wearing an Oakland Raiders football team cap while withdrawing $280 from his account with his wife's car visible in the background. This ATM footage would be the last confirmed sighting of Fisher.

1-01 74TH ST. MCDOWELL

04/09/01 M10:42:07

Last confirmed sighting of Robert Fisher via ATM footage

It took four days for the Arizona Department of Public Safety to send out a state-wide call for Fisher's arrest and six more days for authorities to find the abandoned car and the family dog, a Labrador retriever named Blue, in the Tonto National Forest. In the car was the Oakland Raiders hat that was visible in the ATM surveillance footage. Next to the car was a pile of human excrement.

Although his car was located, no other sign of Fisher would ever be found. The search of the Tonto National Forrest would prove futile in part because of the extensive caves – some of them so vast that investigators knew searching the caves would prove too dangerous. Also in the vicinity was the Fort Apache Reservation, which investigators did not search. First, it is a sovereign nation where Arizona state police are not invited. Second, the reservation is 1.6 million acres, which is more than twice the size of Rhode

Island.

On July 19, arrest warrants charging Fisher with triple homicide and arson were issued, while the United States District Court for the District of Arizona – a federal body – named him as a fugitive. A year later, on July 29, 2002, the FBI placed Fisher on their 10 Most Wanted List, where he remained until November 3, 2021. He was removed from the list because the list is designed to increase public awareness so that potential leads might be phoned in. But the 20 years of publicity had not turned up any valuable leads, so he was taken off the list, although he is certainly still wanted. He is the only one ever named as a person of interest or a suspect in the case.

Police recovering Fisher's car

Despite the triple homicide charge, some are convinced it was actually a triple-homicide-suicide given much of the circumstantial evidence, including the point that no trace of Robert Fisher, who would now, in 2022, be 60-years-old, has ever been verified by anyone in 20 years since the man disappeared. Bolstering this theory, it was reported by Ann Ryman in The

Arizona Republic that Fisher's "friends say he threatened suicide once before, three years before the murders, while despondent over his marriage."

Many others, however, believe Fisher is still alive and that he meticulously executed his plan to eliminate his family and start a new life. A former neighbor of the Fishers in Scottsdale said that he had been on a hunting trip with Fisher in the same area the car was found, the trip occurring just prior to the murders. And while it is difficult to disappear without a trace, leaving no clues besides an abandoned car with the family dog sitting nearby indicates a careful plan to disappear may have been executed to perfection.

All that planning and suicide? At this point, twenty years later, it's still anyone's guess. It's telling that J.D. Duran, the initial lead investigator on the case, said in a Channel 12 interview, "I lean that he's still alive." In contrast, the current investigator declared, "He went off into the woods and committed suicide."

Police began to investigate what could have motivated Fisher to annihilate his family. Robert Fisher was (or is) a former firefighter and Navy corpsman with a history of depression and marital troubles. He and Mary Cooper were married in 1987, and although the family presented publicly as happy and loving, multiple neighbors reported hearing explosive arguments regularly. The marriage was seemingly disintegrating, and allegedly it was common to hear berating messages, such as, "you're worthless" and "you'll never amount to anything" coming from the Fisher home. The night of the murders, neighbors reportedly heard an altercation around 10 p.m. It became clear that at the time of his family's deaths, Robert Fisher was severely distraught by the possibility that his marriage was about to end after years of marital strife.

Robert Fisher had his setbacks. The first and perhaps the most impactful was his parents' divorce, which occurred when he was 15. He and his sisters went to live with his father, but a friend of

Fisher's later said he was "very bitter" about the family splitting up. Psychology experts surmised that one of his biggest fears was having the same trauma occur to his family. Fisher was likely triggered by his wife telling friends a divorce was imminent just weeks before she was found dead in the destroyed home.

After high school, Robert Fisher joined the U.S. Navy and attempted to join the Navy SEALS, but was turned down. Although not an outdoorsman as a child, he took up hunting and fishing with zeal and dedication in his early adulthood. However, he sometimes exhibited odd and impulsive behavior on outings, such as the time he smeared elk blood all over his face and the times he snuck up behind picnicking families and emptied his gun, firing into the air. He was also controlling and impulsive at home, tossing both his son and daughter out of a boat in a "sink or swim" lesson.

His cruelty extended to animals, as he reportedly once shot a stray dog and staged an event to look like he was protecting his own dog when no such threat existed. Fisher was also unfaithful to his wife, having admitted to his pastor that he spent the night with a sex worker shortly before the death of his family.

After his stint in the Navy, Robert Fisher lived in California and became a firefighter. But he was injured on the job and his sore back, from then on, gave him an odd posture when he walked with his chest pushed forward. He moved his family to Arizona and then took up a series of healthcare technician jobs, including surgical assistant, respiratory therapist, and catheter technician.

Despite the passage of twenty years, the loss of the Fisher family is still felt by many. Former neighbor, Lori Greenbeck, remains haunted by the case. The explosion of April 10, 2001, shook homes a half-mile in all directions, but the loss of Mary and the two children have left unhealed emotional scars. She says she loved Mary Fisher and her daughter's best friend was Brittney Fisher.

While there are some tragedies where no one has a clue what is coming around the corner, the Robert Fisher case is even more haunting because the clues were there. The marriage was well known to be darkly dysfunctional. Fisher was known to be brooding, controlling, and angry. Friends and family knew Mary to have been about to file for divorce, the most dangerous juncture for victims of domestic abuse.

Hindsight, of course, is 20-20. Clearly, the clues of an impending homicide were not loud enough, clear enough, consistent enough for alarms to sound. Before the murders and explosion, Robert Fisher went to work, walked the dog, and presumably, said hello to his neighbors. There was no domestic violence on a level that seemed to indicate a triple homicide was around the corner. The couple had even tried marriage counseling with a senior pastor at the Scottsdale Baptist Church.

Hundreds of hundreds of leads have been phoned in concerning possible Robert Fisher sightings over the years, especially after the case was featured on *The Hunt With John Walsh.* But none of the leads, including one phoned in from Vancouver by the Canadian Royal Mounted Police, have ever panned out.

Dead or alive, the trail has gone cold, swallowed up by the cloudless Arizona night.

ROBERT WILLIAM FISHER

Unlawful Flight to Avoid Prosecution - First Degree Murder (3 Counts), Arson of an Occupied Structure

Photograph taken in 1999   Photograph taken in 1997   Age-Enhanced photograph   Age-Enhanced photograph

FBI Most Wanted poster with age-enhanced photos of how Fisher may look now

WILLIAM HUFF

Sierra Vista, Arizona, a once slumbering neighborhood about 75 miles southeast of the growing city of Tuscon, is, by definition, a bedroom community to the Fort Huachuca military base and was, in 1967, a blooming, young retirement enclave.

But the peaceful community was rocked hard, some say forever, by two grisly murders that forced people to re-examine the definition of what defines a serial killer.

Among the factors that increased the fear percolating in Sierra Vista in April 1967 was the fact that this was the first-time murders occurred in the community that involved mutilation, the point that the victims were very young, innocent girls, and the horrifying note the killer sent to police after the first victim was found. This note taunted the police and stated that there would be another victim, even defining that victim by age, gender and location. In the note, the killer also gave himself a chilling nickname, indicating he was taking pride in his crime. He called himself the Phantom.

The note is brazen, ghoulish, frightening, and criminally naive. It warns the police that the author will never be found because he is a gray-haired older man, a red flag to experienced law enforcement suggesting he was more than likely a young man trying to mislead investigators.

Here is the note in its entirety, including parts that were underlined and given multiple exclamation marks:

I am the Phantom.

You have found my first victim. My next one lives on Steffen, a 9 year old girl. I don't live in Sierra Vista. Nobody knows where my hangout is. But one clue is where the sun set the fastest, you shall see three trees. Sure, I am an old man with gray hair, but you'll never find me. There are thousands of old men now. Anyone that fit my description (ha! ha!) but watch out!!

MY NEXT VICTIM LIVES ON STEFFEN STREET 9 ½ yrs old (fools!!)

The Phantom

This note arrived after the first victim disappeared for three days, a seven-year-old named Cindy Clelland. Her sister, Darlene, almost 50 years later described her as a typical "happy" young child with every promise of a long life ahead of her. Her family assumed she had spent the night at a friend's somewhere, but when she did not return, the search was undertaken. Police brought articles of clothing to the child's mother for identification and then, three days later, found her nude, mutilated body in a patch of desert on the military base. Horrifyingly, investigators found signs of sexual assault.

Cindy Clelland

In an interview with CBS 5, Sierra Vista Police Chief, David Santor, said, "this particular type of crime was totally foreign to Sierra Vista." He commented that Cindy's murder changed the town forever.

She was found April 30, 1967. A week later, the gruesome note arrived. It shows emotional denial, a taunting sense of victory, even a sense that the killer was having fun. Police knew it was the writing of an immature man but did not know the note's author was all of 16-years of age.

For the police, the search was on and the hunt was extensive, involving state and city police, as well as the FBI. But the search was also futile, and before they could stop the child killer, six-year-old Janelle Haynes turned up missing on June 22. Under similar circumstances, her lifeless body was also found, mutilated and half-nude in an empty stretch of desert near the military base.

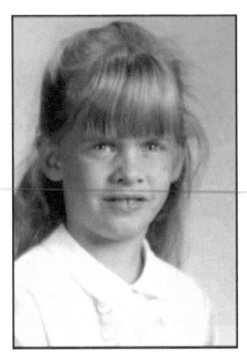

Janelle Haynes

Breaking the case, police matched the handwriting of the taunting note to the writing of high school student William Huff. They soon learned Huff had a history that included behavior similar to other sex offenders and serial killers. He was known to have killed cats – and killing pets is a place many murders get their start. A neighbor had also accused Huff of entering her home. During the break-in, the neighbor suspected Huff had molested her young daughter.

Huff was arrested and soon confessed to what he had done. He was sentenced to 15-years imprisonment for the first murder and 40-years for the second. He served 48 years behind bars, where his prison record was exemplary. He got an education while in prison, kept out of trouble, and was released to a half-way house, where he was put on house arrest. He wore an ankle bracelet, but was free to roam the neighborhood, where he was known to take bicycle rides and go on walks.

Huff at the time of his arrest

The state did not inform neighbors a convicted pedophile and killer was living amongst them, and, unsurprisingly, it caused an uproar. Members of the Clemency Board, which grants parole, were challenged for their decision to let him out of jail.

Just three years later, he was thrown back in jail for breaking parole after his girlfriend's eight-year-old daughter was found sleeping on the couch where Huff was staying. She was found there during a surprise visit from his parole officer. According to an investigative report by Morgan Loew for CBS 5, it appears that the girlfriend was unaware Huff had been imprisoned for crimes against children at the time she brought her young girl into the home. Surprisingly, she would later appear before the Clemency Board to defend Huff.

What defines a psychopathic personality? Like any personality description, it takes multiple indicators to create a complete picture. A fabric of behaviors, emotional functioning and thought patterns shape how a killer thinks and behaves. But where the legal system is concerned is the answer to the question: Will the psychopathic personality in question strike again?

Standardized definitions of serial killers point to people who kill three people or more on multiple occasions and generally take pleasure in the killing – they think it is fun. There is a cooling-off period between murders, which separates a serial killer from a mass murderer, who kills multiple victims in one incident. The cooling-off period also suggests they know they should go into hiding and points to the grim truth that they have time to think about what they did and found themselves unwilling or unable to stop. They often require an emotional cooling down time, having experienced heightened emotions during the killing.

Though Huff only got the opportunity to extinguish two young lives, there is every indication that he had the intention to do it again; therefore, this publication feels it is appropriate to classify William Huff as a serial killer.

When Police Chief David Santor was asked whether or not he believed William Huff is a serial killer, he replied, without hesitation, "absolutely."

No specific recipe of emotional functioning or brain patterns make up a serial killer, and, indeed, part of the profile includes what is called a "unique motivation" for killing others. This "unique" aspect of the killing suggests motivation that comes from some twisted fantasy or paranoia. The motivation, in other words, is not circumstantially tied to an event that universally triggers anger – think road rage or the neighbor's dog barking. The motivation, instead, comes from within, from a dark brew of psychological malfeasance.

The gruesome nature of the killing is also an indicator that the murderer is pathologically tied to the crime, as it points to someone playing with the results of the murder – providing his or herself with a behavioral trophy of sorts, as if mutilation was a behavioral form of gloating.

Huff after parole violation

But all this adds up to the same question that faces the legal system. After 48-years in prison was it a wise decision to allow William Huff to be released? By then, he appeared to be a rational man. He told the Clemency Board he had no intention of violating the law again – a somewhat clinical way of defining his personal affectation. Those who decided to release him were hopeful by this time Huff would have "aged out of crime" - a theory in criminology that suggests an offender's propensity to commit crimes decreases with age.

In an exchange that showed his true nature, a news reporter asked him on camera if he understood why neighbors were concerned about his presence among them, Huff said, yes he understood.

"Why is that?" the reporter asked.

"Because of what happened to me." Huff replied.

"You mean, because of what you did," the reporter said.

"Yeah, yeah, yeah," Huff said.

JODI ARIAS

The media frenzy surrounding the murder of 31-year-old Mesa, Arizona, resident Travis Victor Alexander at the hands of his 28-year-old girlfriend Jodi Arias, reveals one of humankind's purest fascinations.

Murder, of course, is a core mystery in the annals of human behavior, even when the motivations are clearly understood. But a murderess who is young, pretty, and tragically detached from reality, opens a deeper set of vicarious curiosity. We see the advantages and the hopeful time-horizon of youth and the opportunities afforded people who are physically attractive. When all of this becomes ultimately violent and self-destructive, a battery of surreal and perplexing questions arise.

Jodi Arias and Travis Alexander

Not only that, but the Jodi Arias trial became a media sensation, with viewers numbering into the millions, according to ratings published by "The Hollywood Reporter." Contributing to the spectacle, this intriguing defendant, like a wisp of smoke, took to the witness stand in her own defense and testified for a total of eighteen days on the witness stand. To many it was clear that Ms. Arias reveled in the fame her crime had provided, evident from the day she asked for makeup while she was grilled in the interrogation room at the police station. Secondly, Ms. Arias seemed purposefully vague and forgetful, sometimes remembering parts of her story she had forgotten and sometimes forgetting parts she remembered. Over the course of three days, she changed her story repeatedly. Not only did all these shenanigans crush her hopes at winning her case, but they kept her preening in front of the jury and the video cameras almost as if she were cast in the role by a movie director instead of by her own defenseless crime.

She gave calculated answers, pausing to think of what to say, then parsing through one word, testing that word, discarding it, then going back to it. She seemed to be writing the script as she went along, rather than giving spontaneous answers that, at least, would seem genuine or honest.

If that weren't enough, a line up of mental health experts testifying for and against Ms. Arias stirred up more questions than they answered. Psychologist Richard Samuels began by declaring Ms. Arias suffered from "acute stress" at the time of the murder, saying she was in a "fight or flight" mode when the killing occurred. Psychotherapist Alyce LaViolette then testified Ms. Arias was the victim of domestic violence, only to be trumped by clinical psychologist Janeen DeMarte who diagnosed Ms. Arias with post-traumatic stress disorder and borderline personality disorder. For the prosecution, psychologist Robert Geffner said, no, she suffered from anxiety disorder and trauma. And, if the jury wasn't confused yet, forensic neurologist Jill Haynes got on the stand and testified that the tests DeMarte had administered were not credible for diagnosing borderline personality disorder, which is a difficult diagnosis to understand.

But a deeper sense of the unreal is at stake here, which is the tendency to misjudge the nature of mental illness. As a society, we often erroneously assume that all those who are mentally ill will be visibly unwell, maybe grisly and unwashed, perhaps even hungry and unhinged. What if you were pretty and well-scrubbed, even smiling and apparently self-assured? We are clearly shocked to see any human being commit a heinously violent crime. But one who is presentable and charming – that doesn't add up. It challenges our expectations of who becomes mentally ill and what mental illness might look like. Mental illness has many faces. Sometimes it comes with a growl and sometimes it comes with a smile.

This even challenges the professionals, apparently. In one dramatic moment, Maricopa County Prosecutor Juan Martinez attempted to discredit Richard Samuel's testimony saying he had a relationship with Ms. Arias because he had said he felt compassion towards her. Mr. Samuels was clearly affronted by the question and stormed back, "I beg your pardon, sir!"

The controversies didn't stop there. Martinez himself seemed overwhelmed by the publicity surrounding the case and the chance of being the ringmaster in the media circus. His grandstanding and badgering witnesses set the bar high for both. He was first accused of "systematically excluding" women and Blacks from the jury, a charge that was ruled invalid by the court. Later, he was charged with harassing witnesses, barking at them, challenging them with staring duels, asserting his authority at every turn.

Mr. Martinez was also charged with taking evidence out of the courtroom, which he did so he could pose with the evidence in photo opportunities with the media.

This media circus of a trial, surrounded a very grisly murder that eventually ended with a sentence of life without parole for Ms. Arias.

The victim was Arias' boyfriend Travis Victor Alexander, a popular man who was a salesman and a motivational speaker, who worked for Pre-Paid Legal Services. He had been missing for several days in early June 2008, before friends went to his apartment to find him. They found him curled up in the bottom of his shower, stabbed 27-29 times and with his throat cut from ear to ear. He had also been shot in the head with a .25-caliber handgun, which was never recovered, although, significantly, a gun of that caliber was reported stolen from her grandparents on May 28, less than a week before the murder occurred.

A shell casing was found at the murder scene and, in very incriminating fashion, a recently purchased digital camera was found in a washing machine on site. The camera's memory card contained nude photos of both Arias and the victim, who had sex just before the murder, and photos of Travis Alexander's bloody body lying in the shower. A handprint matching Arias' was also found in a pool of blood in the bathroom. There were also numerous phone calls traced between Arias and the victim in the hours before his death, and a gas can was found, thought to have been purchased so that Arias would not have to stop for gas on her way to her boyfriend's apartment. With this ploy, she hoped to convince authorities that she could not have driven that far to get to his place from her home in Redding, California.

When you add up all the evidence left at the crime, it would almost seem impossible to imagine that Jodi Arias was simply going about her normal routine from June 4, when the murder took place, until July 15, when she was arrested at her home. She was indicted July 9 and arrested six days later, which allowed her over a month to leave the country or, at least, go into hiding in the United States. She then pleaded not guilty as the media caught wind of the news that an attractive young woman had murdered somebody.

Arias was assigned two county-paid defense attorneys, and the pre-trial motions were filed April 6, 2009, asking the court to move the venue due to media-incited prejudices. That motion was denied, and the court soon ordered a complete psychiatric analysis of the defendant, which held off the start of the trial until December 10, 2012. By the time it was over with sentencing hearings in May 2013, the defense had cost the county more than $3 million.

Although shocking to the general public, Alexander's friends and family had been skeptical of Arias since the beginning of the relationship. She was extremely possessive of Travis, often eavesdropping on his phone calls and snooping through his phone. After catching Arias spying on Alexander, one of his friends, Sky Lovingier Hughes confronted him, saying, "Travis, I'm afraid we're gonna find you chopped up in her freezer." She further told ABC News,"from very early on, she was completely obsessed with him."

Just before his murder, Alexander planned to end his affair with Arias. Although the two were in a sexual relationship, he was reportedly a devout Mormon, and his guilt over their "sins" was looming too large to ignore. According to the book "Picture Perfect: The Jodi Arias Story" by Shana Hogan, "Travis wanted to marry a virginal, pure Mormon girl, and by having sex with him, Jodi eliminated herself as ever being marriage potential for Travis."

When Alexander tried to end the relationship, Arias was desperate to win him back. Travis broke the news to Arias that he wanted to end their relationship and that he no longer wanted her to accompany him on vacation to Mexico; instead, he would be bringing a female friend. Jodi got into her car, allegedly armed with a stolen gun, and began the arduous, almost fourteen-hour drive from Redding to Mesa. Evidence recovered on a camera at the crime scene provided insight into the couple's illicit activities in the last hours of Travis' life.

Camera (left) discovered in Alexander's washing machine containing last photos of him alive

In all likelihood, after Arias realized that she could no longer control her lover, even with sex, she decided that if she couldn't have him, no one could. A bloody fight ensued. Mesa Police Detective Estaban Flores told "20/20", "The first thing I thought {when I arrived at the crime scene} was there was a major struggle in here...That it was deeply personal. Somebody knew him. Somebody wanted him dead...Somebody wanted to make sure that he was dead."

The evidence found at the scene suggests Travis fought desperately for his life. Arias' co-workers reported that her hands were covered in lacerations in the days following the attack.

Alexander's bloody bathroom

Arias claimed innocence to the end, before asking for leniency. In a televised interview soon after her arrest, she said, "A jury won't convict me ever, because I am innocent." At sentencing, however, she admitted her deep grief over what she had done. "Until very recently, I could not imagine standing before you and asking to give me life," she said. However, she said she knew more denials would continue to bring pain to the victim's family.

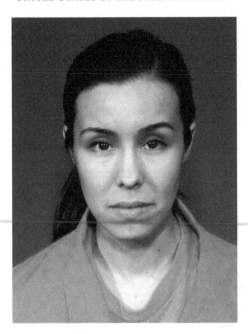

Jodi Arias' mugshot

She began her sentence in the Lumley maximum security facility within the Perryville, Arizona, state prison and has since been moved to a medium-security section of the prison. A re-sentencing trial was held in the early summer of 2015 due to a mistrial at her earlier sentencing. Her prison term was reaffirmed.

JARED LOUGHNER

Mass murderer Jared Lee Loughner, who was diagnosed with paranoid schizophrenia and initially judged incompetent to stand trial, is famously remembered for the mug shot taken the day of his arrest.

This photograph, which was distributed widely through the media the day after the shooting that left six dead and many others wounded, showed a mildly satisfied young man with a closely cropped haircut, looking slightly alien and childishly pleased at what he had just done. The New York Times description of the photograph said Loughner looked "smirking and creepy with hollow eyes ablaze."

Jared Loughner

There is no question that the man in the photo is the embodiment of creepy, a detached, disjointed man disconnected to the circumstances, smiling only hours after a shooting spree that shocked the nation as much for the body count as for the political aspects of the case.

Jared Loughner's target was U.S. Rep. Gabrielle Dee Giffords, a congresswoman he shot in the head at close range. Amazingly Giffords survived the harrowing attack.

Known as Gabby, she was the third woman in Arizona's history to be elected to Congress, a Cornell University graduate. She was also a former Republican who had switched her party affiliation to Democrat in 2000. At the time of the shooting, Giffords was conducting an open constituent meeting at a Safeway grocery store location in Casas Adobes, a community in northern Tucson, Arizona.

Giffords was the first to be shot, but Jared Loughner, born September 10, 1988, 23-years-old at the time of the attack, did not stop there. Firing the 9 mm Glock handgun he had purchased at a Sportsman Warehouse on November 30, 2010, Loughner fatally injured Chief U.S. District Court Judge John Roll and Giffords' congressional aide Gabe Zimmerman. He also fatally injured a nine-year-old girl named Christina-Taylor Green. One victim was injured while fleeing the scene and, paradoxically, another was injured in an attempt to subdue the crazed gunman.

Christina Taylor Green

Rep. Gabrielle Giffords

Federal Judge John Roll

Phyllis Schneck

Gabe Zimmerman

Dorothy Morris

Dorwan Stoddard

Victims of Loughner's attack

Of course, the word "crazed" is the operable word in the case of Jared Loughner. His medical history reveals a classic case of unhinged, untreated schizophrenia, which is marked by paranoid delusions, disorganized thinking, and audible and visual hallucinations that can make it difficult to understand what is real and what is imagined. The illness often gives its victims the idea that they are being controlled by powerful, unknown foes, which tells them what to think or do. Although disruptive outbursts are common, these controlling manifestations rarely dictate specific violence, deriving from overwhelming confusion and deeply felt fears. The ability to follow instructions, to concentrate, and to understand lucid reasoning patterns are disrupted.

No specific hallucinatory commands, such as "go hurt someone", have been reported in the Jared Loughner case, in part because of his initial refusal to submit to psychiatric evaluations. However, Loughner purchased the gun used in the attack more than a month prior to the shooting and ammunition just the morning of the attack. After the shooting, a friend of his found a voice message on an answering machine in which Loughner said, "Me and you had good times... Peace," indicating Loughner knew the difference between right and wrong, between peace and violence. He left another message at his residence that said "Goodbye, friends. Please don't be mad at me," a message that included the words, "I want to make it out alive" after the shooting. This shows he knew what he was doing included the risks to himself, a rudimentary sign of rational thinking.

The shooting took place January 8, 2011 at just after 10:00 a.m., two and a half hours after Loughner purchased ammunition at a Walmart on North Cortaro Road at 7:28 a.m.

Scene of the shooting

Loughner was 23 at the time, an age that will sound predictable to persons with extensive knowledge of schizophrenia. The illness often begins to exert itself in a person's late teens, which is followed by a few years of struggle to remain lucid and in control. Behavioral problems start to escalate and conflicts with friends, family and authority figures arise with growing frequency. Persons with schizophrenia fear the idea that their craziness is permanent or noticeable. As in the Loughner case, persons with schizophrenia often reach for street drugs and alcohol to mitigate the symptoms they cannot understand. Tranquilizers – and there are many street versions of tranquilizers – are often prescribed to persons with schizophrenia, so it is no wonder that young victims turn to drugs and alcohol. This often delays the discovery of the illness, as someone with schizophrenia turns to self-medicating options at the same age as many of their friends begin experimenting with mood and mind-altering substances.

Jared Loughner's behavioral outbursts began when he was

enrolled in Pima Community College. Classmates, professors, campus police, and school administrators became increasingly concerned with his acting out. Eventually, the college suspended Loughner with the stipulation that he could return if he received mental health clearance, meaning that a mental health professional would need to vouch for his ability to control himself. Loughner never sought such an evaluation, choosing, instead, to drop out of college.

His parents, Randy and Amy Loughner, described as very private people, were concerned about Jared's growing irrationality. They attended meetings with college administrators and learned of his outbursts on the campus. They also took to hiding his car keys at night to keep him at home, where they could keep an eye on him.

During this period, Loughner's anti-government ideas came to light, noticed by many of his friends and acquaintances. While the press reported his views as anti-abortion views similar to Tea Party members, psychiatric evaluations discerned his politics were vague and non-specific. One evaluator, Kathryn Olmsted at U.C. Davis, noted that Loughner's views were a confused garble that ranged from pro-Karl Marx to pro-Adolf Hitler. She called them "a toxic jumble of left and right-wing" viewpoints.

Things erupted on January, 8, 2011, when Jared Loughner opened fire, shooting Gabby Giffords first, then firing at random at the crowd. Before it was over, six were dead and thirteen wounded.

Friends were shocked. His high school girlfriend of several months, Kelsey Hawkes, said, "I've always known him as the sweet, caring Jared." Another friend, Tong Shan, said he knew Jared Loughner was "anti-government," but he did not know him to have any violent tendencies. The unknowing friends point to the nefarious, seditious side of schizophrenia. In all likelihood, Jared Loughner, before schizophrenia, was a gentle, caring person. The danger is that, when schizophrenia first hits, its victims have not begun to understand their mind is playing tricks on them, and they have not learned to ignore the inner voices or take responsibility for them. While the majority of people with schizophrenia do not go on to commit violent crimes, a young person who is just beginning to experience symptoms is more vulnerable than someone who better understands their illness and is receiving treatment.

Prior to the shooting, Loughner had become more erratic and anti-social. He was arrested for minor incidents, including possession of marijuana and drug paraphernalia and vandalism, after drawing a stylized "CX" on public property. The "CX" is a cult-like symbol for Christianity. But like politics, Loughner's religious views were also from a grab-bag of random influences, not a coherent or steadfast affiliation.

Following the shooting, Loughner was assigned a public defender whose only line of defense was to help Loughner plead insanity. Two early evaluations judged Loughner incompetent to stand trial. So the state decided to place Loughner on forced medication, which would create a more lucid, rational prisoner they could try in court. This drug regimen was ruled a violation of Loughner's rights since he was presumed innocent until a trial, and as an innocent person, the state had no right to force medication on him. However, a subsequent hearing revealed a loophole and found that Loughner could be sedated to control a prisoner for his own safety or the safety of others. Using this line of reasoning, the state forced Loughner to take the antipsychotic drug risperidone. When all of Arizona's available judges recused themselves from the case due to the death of Judge John Roll, killed by Loughner in the attack, San Diego-based circuit Judge Larry Alan Burns ruled Loughner competent to stand trial on August 7, 2012. In a deal to avoid the death penalty, Loughner pleaded guilty to 19 counts.

Unlike some states, Arizona law does not give defendants the option of pleading "innocent by reason of insanity." It only allows for "guilty, but insane." In November 2012, Loughner was sentenced to life plus 140 years in prison. He remains in prison today, not eligible for parole.

ROBERT SPANGLER

Serial killers form a gruesome stereotype in the mind of the public supported by horror films, campfire stories, and dire warnings by parents afraid of what might happen if their kids stay out too late.

These serial killers, the ones that haunt the back of our minds, are unwashed, unshaved, uncouth. They have untrimmed fingernails that are crusted over with mud. They frequent seedy bars and hang out with low-life characters. They look menacing. They thrive in the shadowlands and only come out of their homes at night.

What if none of that were true? What about well-educated, well-dressed, charismatic community members who join the local theater group, attend parent-teacher conferences, take an extra job at a local radio station and think a day off is best spent hiking in the great outdoors, reveling in the marvels of Mother Nature?

This almost sound like the well-rounded renaissance man, who favors natural food restaurants, herbal tea and sandals, a free-spirit, perhaps.

Not quite. Robert Spangler was an in-touch-with nature type, born in January 1933. He lived in Littleton, Colorado, in the 1970s and was well-known in the community for his local radio show and his participation in community events. He worked in various fields, but succeeded in the bulk of his career as a human resources and public relations man, who was charismatic and adept at public speaking. But, he had a very dark side, too. The problem was, he was smart enough to get away with a triple homicide for

22-years. His targets, consistently, were people he was close to. His continued freedom made him so arrogant that he committed a fourth murder; thankfully, that murder would finally put him on the radar of Arizona police.

Robert Spangler

It even looked like Spangler was a loving, doting family man to police at first. They were called to the Spangler home on the morning of December 30, 1978, where they found the Spangler children, David, 17, and Susan, 15, both dead of gunshot wounds, the boy shot in the back, the girl shot in the chest. Slumped over a typewriter in a basement room was Robert Spangler's first wife, Nancy, 45, a suicide note conveniently found in the typewriter, signed by Nancy's initials.

The weapon was in plain sight, a .38-caliber handgun. Nancy had died from a bullet wound with the entrance point high on her forehead, the angle of the bullet about 60 degrees above level, the bullet traveling through the top of her brain. Forensic evidence would conclude she had fired – or at least – held the murder weapon.

Nancy Spangler   David Spangler   Susan Spangler

Police also found gunpowder residue on Robert Spangler's hand, but the grieving husband, who said the couple were having marital problems, also said he had found the gun on the floor and handled it before calling the police.

And the police had to believe him. There was no evidence to allow them to charge Robert Spangler with any crime, even if he said he had been having an affair with a co-worker named Sharon Cooper. After two polygraphs that were inconclusive, Robert Spangler was declared uninvolved, as the case was ruled a murder/suicide. Nancy Spangler had shot her children, suffocating her son David to death when the shot fired proved not to be fatal. Then, the coroner concluded, she wrote her suicide note and shot herself in the head.

Robert Spangler grieved, then he married Sharon Cooper seven months later. The couple enjoyed hiking so much so that they became avid fans of the Grand Canyon, one of the treasures of the great west. They were so involved with hiking that Sharon even wrote a book about their hiking experiences before leaving her husband in 1988. As the marriage was dissolving, she told friends she thought her husband was "out to get her."

Years later, on October 2, 1994, Robert Spangler would make an effort to reconnect with his second wife, only the visit did not go well. That day, Robert found Sharon unresponsive on the floor of her house next to a bottle of Tylenol. Her death was not investigated, although she died that day of an overdose. Spangler was the last person to see her alive.

Sharon Cooper

That effort to reconnect with Sharon was, perhaps, a logical turn of events given what happened in April 1993. Apparently, in an attempt to rekindle their marriage, Spangler was hiking in the Grand Canyon with Donna Sunding, his third wife. They had moved in together in August 1990, Sunding an older woman who was an aerobics instructor and a grandmother with many grandkids and several children.

Donna Sunding was also afraid of heights and not an avid hiker, as was Sharon Cooper. Nevertheless, the couple decided on a Grand Canyon trip to have some quality time together, and it was there that Donna Sunding met her death. On April 11, 1993, Robert Spangler showed up at a ranger station in the national park and calmly told Rangers that his third wife had fallen to her death. She was close to the edge of a 160-foot high canyon wall, and he took a few steps away to take her picture. When he turned around with the camera in his hand, he said, his wife had disappeared.

Donna Sunding

Donna's death earned Spangler some national fame, as several news outlets interviewed the grieving widow, who was at that point championing the cause of safe hiking, warning people to stay away from the edges.

Stay away from Spangler might have been better advice.

After Sunding's death, National Park Special Agents began their investigation. Despite the fact that the hiking trail to Horseshoe Mesa, where the body was found, is known to be deadly, agents found the situation suspicious. Those who were close to Donna knew she suffered from vertigo and told investigators it was unlikely that she would willingly go close enough to the edge of a vast cliff that she could tumble off. Suspicions were solidified after law enforcement in Arizona learned of the strange circumstances surrounding the death of Robert's family in Colorado. For the next six years, various law enforcement agencies, including the FBI and National Center for the Analysis of Violent Crime, built a case against Spangler. However, without his confession, hope began to fade that justice would ever be served.

A glimmer of hope came in 1999 when a local woman contacted authorities to tell them she had just received a letter from Spangler. In the letter, he said he had terminal cancer. Law enforcement knew the truth was slipping away with Spangler.

Several law enforcement agencies set up a meeting to discuss cases that had gone cold and decided to test Robert Spangler with interrogation techniques designed to make use of a psychological assessment assembled after putting all the known facts on the table.

Spangler confessed he had pushed his third wife off the high Arizona cliff, walking up to her, a woman afraid of heights, while she was facing him. Her body tumbled 140 feet, then came to rest 160 feet below the trail. The cause of death included lacerations, contusions, brain trauma, a neck broken in several places, multiple fractures of her legs and lower torso, broken ribs, a crushed chest.

Bottom of the trail where Sunding's body was discovered

And how did the investigators catch Spangler? Along with their psychological profile, which determined how they would question him, authorities had interviewed an Arizona woman who had met Spangler on the trail. It turns out, Spangler, after pushing his wife off the cliff, returned many times to the Grand Canyon with friends on subsequent hiking trips – kind of a celebrity with one wife writing a book about hiking there and another wife plunging to her death there, too.

Investigators played on the killer's hubris to get him talking. According to a report by ABC News, Spangler "agreed to confess because he wanted FBI profilers to explain to him why he was so good at killing." He would also claim to be "different" from other serial killers because he was "interesting." Despite an obvious desire to seek attention for his crimes, it would seem that his psychological needs were contradictory. He wanted fame for his crimes, but then, after confessing he had shot his two children and his first wife, then pushed his third wife to her death, he wrote the police a letter asking them to "minimize" the case when talking to news outlets, because he didn't want to sully his reputation in the community.

It was a bit late for that. Spangler was dubbed "The Widower" and featured in several popular crime shows. He died in a maximum-security medical center in Springfield, Missouri, on August 5, 2001, while serving a life sentence without parole. In his confessions, he admitted that he lured his first wife into the basement by saying he had a Christmas "surprise" for her. The overdose of his second wife has still never been investigated.

CHRISTOPHER MATTHEW CLEMENTS

On April 20, 2012, young Isabel Mercedes Celis trundled off to bed at 11:00 p.m., late for a youngster, but not uncommon or unsafe for a child under the devoted, watchful eye of her family, including father and mother Sergio and Becky Celis of the Garden District in north-central Tucson. Her loving parents gave her kisses and hugs, tucked her into bed and turned out the light. They never saw their daughter alive again.

Isabel Celis

Whether or not 38-year-old sex offender Christopher Mathew Clements reached through Isabel Celis' bedroom window late at night to snatch the girl or lured her to climb through the window with promises of some kind is not known at this point. However, his involvement in her murder is crystal clear. Whatever the case, suddenly young Isabel was gone and her parents quickly called the police, which triggered a massive hunt for the girl that turned into church prayer meetings, community fund drives, and outpouring of sympathy from all corners of the city. The vigils, searches, meetings, prayers would span more than two years, until authorities found her and identified her buried remains after Clements led investigators to her burial place.

Tragically, by then, the killings involved a second victim, another young girl, 13-year-old Maribel Victoria Gonzalez, who disappeared as she was walking to a friend's house in the same neighborhood of Tuscon in June 2014. Her body was found in a barren stretch of desert northwest of the city near Avra Valley and Trico Roads three days after she disappeared. Soon afterward, Clements told investigators he knew where Isabel Celis was buried, and the spot turned out only yards from where Maribel had been found.

Maribel Gonzales

Clements at the time told investigators he had nothing to do with the disappearance or death of these girls, he just happened to know where Isabel Celis' body could be found – and how he happened to know this is still undisclosed at this point. The two separate first-degree murder trials are to be held in early 2022 with the trial for Gonzales' death to begin April 19 – expected to last twelve days – while the trial for Celis' will commence May 24, 2022, a trial expected to run for two weeks.

While no one can proclaim Clements' guilt at this point, where we are leaning is obvious. Clements has pleaded not guilty to all 22 felony charges, which include kidnapping, first degree murder and sexual exploitation of a minor with nothing short of life imprisonment as a potential outcome for each trial. On April 21, 2021, the Pima County Attorney's Office announced it would not seek the death penalty for Clements, a deal that is commonly struck when a defendant trades clemency for information, in this case, leading authorities to the burial spot where Celis was found. But journalists recently uncovered an extremely chilling photograph, which Shaley Sanders of KOLD News 13 described by saying Clements admitted the photograph was one of him looking in the rearview mirror of his car at a small child looking up towards the mirror in the back seat. The photograph shows a forehead and hairline of a man with one eye covered by sunglasses. Next to his cheek is the small face of a child peering plaintively towards Clements or the mirror. It looks like a girl

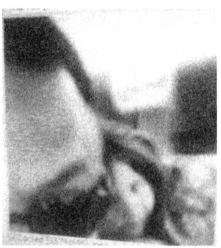

Unfocused image of Clements and unknown child

with soft, round cheeks, her head covered by a coat or a blanket. Is it Isabel or some other young girl? That is also unclear.

What has been revealed is Clements' long rap sheet, which began when he was a minor and started with a sexual offence – two counts of unlawful penetration with a foreign object, which occurred when Clements was 16-years old, living in Oregon. This marked him at that early age as a sex offender. He was sentenced to 18 months imprisonment and ten years of community supervision with the stipulation that he register as a sex offender wherever he lived for the rest of his life. This was a requirement he failed to do on several occasions, a clear indication that he intended to strike again.

After this, Clements' rap sheet includes burglary, identity theft and assault, as well as other sex offences.

In King County, Washington, Clements pleaded guilty to a charge of felony assault, for which he was slapped on the wrist with a year of probation. This occurred in July 2002 and in November he was charged with identity theft and obstructing a police officer. He pleaded guilty in December and was sentenced to another year of probation.

In 2006, Clements was arrested for felony theft – he was convicted for that – and several misdemeanors, including telephonic harassment and violation of a protective order. By October 2006, he was arrested in Florida for failing to register as a sex offender, which concluded with another probation sentence.

On and on. Clements again failed to register as a sex offender when he returned to Oregon in September 2007 and again, when he moved to Tucson, where he was arrested in October, a month after his sex offender registration dodge in Oregon. In Tucson, a police officer took him in finding it suspicious that he pulled trash out of a public trash can. In the incident, Clements drove away and the police followed, pulling him over due to growing suspicions about his behavior. When they questioned him, however, Clements twice gave the officers fake names, which was discovered when they looked at his Oregon drivers' license.

Clements was convicted for failure to register as a sex offender in Arizona in March 2009 and sentenced to 46 months in prison and five years of supervised release. That done, he appealed the case and was let out of prison on a technicality, arguing that he did not have to register as the Sex Offender Registration and Notification Act went into effect in 2006, after his original sex offense had occurred, so it did not apply to him. With that, he was let out of jail.

He moved to an apartment within two miles of the places where the two girls were last seen.

At the time he was questioned by the FBI regarding his involvement in Celias' disappearance, Clements was already in

Maricopa County Jail for unrelated charges. In an interview with ABC15, one of his victims related the extreme lengths Clements and his female accomplice went to in their burglary schemes. The woman, who wished to remain unnamed, says that she had recently lost her daughter to cancer and received a cancer diagnosis herself when Clements targetted her. An unknown caller posing as a FedEx delivery person claimed that the woman had mail from a cancer hospital that needed to be picked up. The woman alleged that she was gone less than ten minutes, and in that time, Clements entered her home and stole thousands of dollars of jewelry. Although frustrated with her situation, she expressed, "when I see what he's capable of doing-- jewelry can be replaced, those littler girls' lives cannot."

While we must presume even the offenders accused of the most repulsive crimes, innocent until convicted in court, it's undeniable that the mountain of evidence piling up against Clements will be difficult for even the best defense team to refute. A report by KOLD News revealed damaging evidence, including a container recovered buried in Clements' backyard that had Isabel's middle name, Mercedes, on homework and a young child's sweater. Upon seizure of his electronic devices, police found despicable photos and searches. In addition to child pornography, the phrase "Isabel Celis sexy" was found, solidifying that this accused murderer is, without a doubt, a pedophile. While still just circumstantial, Tuscon.com reported that a man matching Clements' description had come by the Celis home prior to Isabel's disappearance to inquire about a car of a make that Clements is known to have purchased. The article further documented that the grand jury was presented with evidence that Christopher Clements spent $110 on an extensive car detailing service the morning Isabel was discovered missing.

Further incriminating Clements, phone records prove that his cellphone pinged off the towers for the desert location where the bodies were found on the dates that both Isabel Celis and Maribel

Gonzales went missing. The day after Isabel was reported missing and his phone pinged in the desert, Clements canceled his phone service. However, the most damning piece of evidence came in the form of DNA analysis that placed Clements in contact with Maribel's body. The DNA is likely how police finally connected Clements to that case.

During FBI interviews Clements also expressed that he is willing to lead the authorities to the murder weapon on the condition that he is offered complete immunity and released to his family. Unsurprisingly to anyone with knowledge of our legal system, the FBI is unwilling to release this convicted sex offender suspected of multiple child murders. Therefore there is a chance that no one will ever know the truth of what happened. As his trial unfolds, it is believed that he will testify. Hopefully, his trial and testimony will provide more answers.

Executing Christopher Mathew Clements is off the table, but he might die in prison before his natural life expires. At one of his hearings, Clements went into court sporting a fresh black eye. Prisoners with nothing to lose have been known to murder cell mates who confess they engaged in sex with a minor for no other reason than they don't want to be seen in the company of a pedophile.

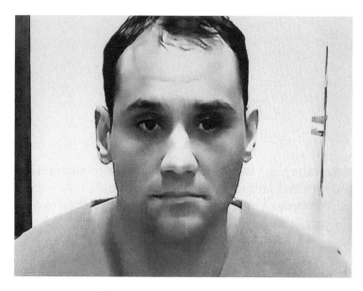

Clements with a black eye in court

According to a staff writer at KOLD News, "In a letter to his fiance, Clements claimed there was a total of four bodies buried in that desert area outside of Tucson. Authorities believe two of the four are Isabel and Maribel. They do not know who the other two are." In the coming months, the public can only hope that the trial of Christopher Clements brings answers, and perhaps even some closure, to the families of his victims.

THANK YOU!

If you've taken the time to reach this far I want to sincerely thank you for your support and I hope you enjoyed this book. If you could take 30 more seconds of your time to leave a review on Amazon at the below link I would greatly appreciate it:

https://www.amazon.com/gp/product/B09S34HBBM/
ref=dbs_a_def_rwt_hsch_vapi_taft_p1_i2

As my way of thanking you for your support, I'd love to send you a free copy of the next ebook or audiobook in this series. If you'd like a free copy of the latest book in the *United States of True Crime* series, please send an email to freebooks@truecrimepublishingcompany.com or visit www.truecrimepublishingcompany.com and fill out the form to become part of our launch team and receive future books for free.

ALSO BY ASHLEY HUDSON

Check out the entire *United States of True Crime* Series on Amazon. A new volume will be released every other month until all 50 states are complete:

https://www.amazon.com/dp/B09M3ZXV1Y?
binding=kindle_edition&ref=dbs_dp_rwt_sb_pc_tukn

COPYRIGHT

Digital Edition February 2022 ISBN: 978-1-957059-06-8
Paperback ISBN: 978-1-957059-07-5
Hardcover ISBN: 978-1-957059-08-2

Printed in the United States of America

Made in the USA
Coppell, TX
15 September 2023

21600538R00056